Celebrating Failure

Great

Sports Fails

Grace Campbell

Lerner Publications ◆ Minneapolis

for Myles, my biggest fan

Lerner Publications Company
An imprint of Lerner Publishing Group, Inc.
241 First Avenue North
Minneapolis, MN 55401 USA

For reading levels and more information, look up this title at www.lernerbooks.com.

Main body text set in Adrianna Regular.
Typeface provided by Chank.

Library of Congress Cataloging-in-Publication Data

Names: Campbell, Grace, 1993– author.
Title: Great sports fails / Grace Campbell.
Description: Minneapolis : Lerner Publications, [2020] | Series: Searchlight books. Celebrating failure | Includes bibliographical references and index.
Identifiers: LCCN 2019013118 (print) | ISBN 9781541577367 (library binding : alk. paper)
Subjects: LCSH: Sports—History—Juvenile literature. | Sports upsets—Juvenile literature.
Classification: LCC GV571 C35 2020 (print) | LCC GV571 (ebook) | DDC 796—dc23

LC record available at https://lccn.loc.gov/2019013118
LC ebook record available at https://lccn.loc.gov/2019980632

Manufactured in the United States of America
1-46758-47749-6/12/2019

Contents

Chapter 1

THE COMEBACK . . . 4

Chapter 2

LIVING IN INFAMY . . . 8

Chapter 3

MISMANAGED, RIGGED, AND DISGRACED . . . 16

Chapter 4

THE TWELFTH MAN . . . 22

Glossary • 30
Learn More about Sports Fails • 31
Index • 32

THE COMEBACK

In the locker room during halftime at the 1993 American Football Conference wild card game, the Houston Oilers were eager to celebrate their 28–3 lead. Quarterback Warren Moon urged his teammates to stay on guard during the second half. With thirty minutes to play, their victory over the Buffalo Bills wasn't guaranteed.

Houston Oilers safety Bubba McDowell returns an interception for a touchdown in the 1993 AFC wild card game. The score gave the Oilers a 35–3 lead.

This play, which came after a botched field goal attempt, was one in a series of second-half mistakes by the Oilers.

Houston scored again early in the third quarter. They extended their lead to 35–3. No team had ever come back from that far behind, and the Oilers knew it. They began to relax just as the Bills found their second wind. Moon and his teammates turned the ball over on interceptions and fumbles. Meanwhile, their defense appeared helpless against the Bills. Buffalo charged back to tie the game and send it into overtime.

The Oilers got the ball first in the sudden-death overtime period, but Moon threw another costly interception. The Bills marched downfield to kick the game-winning field goal. They had staged the biggest comeback in NFL history. The Oilers could only watch Buffalo celebrate, wondering how they'd let victory slip away.

Failure Is Part of the Game

In sports, almost every mistake has an immediate result. One team's loss is another's victory. When a player fails, it's just one moment and one loss in a long career. Mistakes are a necessary part of sports. No player or team can be perfect. Often failures have helped to shape the world of sports.

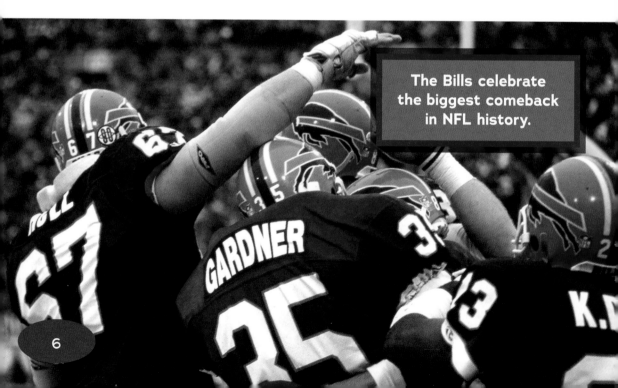

The Bills celebrate the biggest comeback in NFL history.

The Road to Failure

At the 1993 Wimbledon finals, Jana Novotná was up against Steffi Graf. Novotná took a big lead in the third and deciding set. She was just a few points from victory. Then she began to fall apart. She missed serves. She hit volleys into the net. Graf stormed back in a furious comeback to steal the match and the title. Five years later, Novotná finally won Wimbledon, defeating Nathalie Tauziat.

Jana Novotná reaches for a shot during the 1993 Wimbledon finals.

7

Chapter 2

LIVING IN INFAMY

It's easy to blame one mistake for a loss. An athlete who fails in a spectacular way often becomes a scapegoat. Fans and media may ignore a team's other flaws, focusing on that one moment of failure. While these players failed on a global stage, the successes they needed to get there proved their talent.

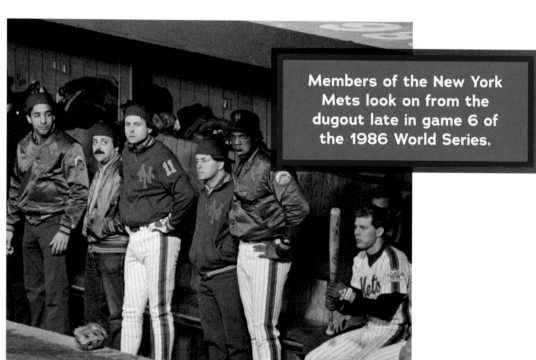

Members of the New York Mets look on from the dugout late in game 6 of the 1986 World Series.

Right through the Legs

It was the tenth inning in the sixth game of the 1986 World Series. The Boston Red Sox led 5–3 with two outs. They were one out away from winning the championship for the first time in almost seventy years. New York Mets outfielder Mookie Wilson slapped a ground ball toward first base, where Bill Buckner stood waiting.

Boston first baseman Bill Buckner became a scapegoat after missing a simple ground ball.

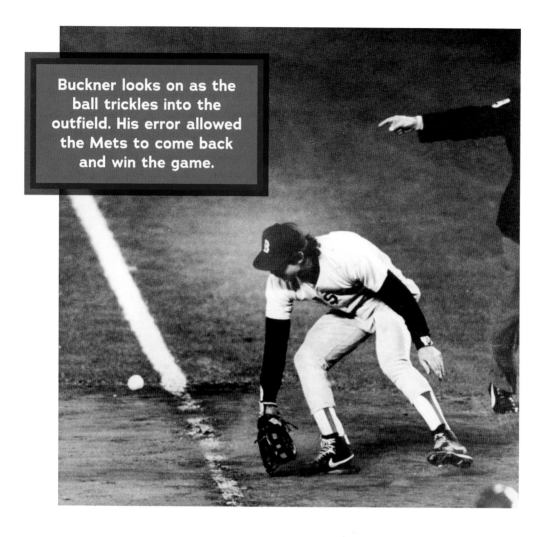

Buckner looks on as the ball trickles into the outfield. His error allowed the Mets to come back and win the game.

It looked like an easy play. But the ball bounced over Buckner's glove and rolled through his legs past first base. The Mets scored and ended up winning the game—and the series. Even though plenty of Red Sox players contributed to the loss, Buckner's failure stood out above all.

Buckner became the scapegoat of the team. The Red Sox released him the following year. He returned to the team briefly in 1990. Fans welcomed him back warmly, having forgiven him. But Buckner and his mistake live on in baseball history.

Buckner walks off the field as Boston fans look on in disbelief.

A Van de Veldian Error

The 1999 British Open Championship was played at the Carnoustie Golf Club in Scotland, nicknamed Car-nasty for its treacherous weather. No one expected a relatively unknown French golfer, Jean Van de Velde, ranked 152nd in the world, to rise to the top of the leaderboard.

Jean Van de Velde's second place finish in the 1999 British Open was by far his best career showing in a major.

Van de Velde removes his shoes and tries to retrieve his ball from a water hazard.

Van de Velde led by a commanding three strokes headed to the final hole. He had been playing aggressively all week, taking chances that had been paying off well. But on his third shot he landed in a water hazard that proved too difficult to escape. Standing in knee-deep water, Van de Velde decided to take the drop and return to the rough. But then he hit the ball into a sand trap.

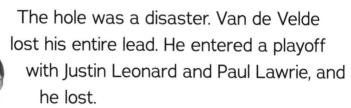

The hole was a disaster. Van de Velde lost his entire lead. He entered a playoff with Justin Leonard and Paul Lawrie, and he lost.

His name has become synonymous with last-minute breakdowns, even with victory in sight. But Van de Velde has overcome his fantastic loss. He says that he wouldn't change a thing about the way he played that day.

Van de Velde celebrates after making a putt that sent him to a playoff at the 1999 British Open.

The Road to Failure

At the 2006 Winter Olympics in Turin, Italy, Lindsey Jacobellis was a clear favorite in snowboard cross. But on the second-to-last jump of the course, the twenty-year-old Jacobellis couldn't contain her excitement. She celebrated certain gold with a method grab. But the trick went wrong. Jacobellis fell and wasn't able to get back up until after Tanja Frieden sailed smoothly past the finish line. Jacobellis didn't see a win in that event at the 2010, 2014, or 2018 Olympics either. Yet she maintained her spot as the world's dominant female snowboarder, with plenty of other medals under her belt.

Lindsey Jacobellis falls at the 2006 Winter Olympic snowboard cross event. Her tumble cost her a gold medal.

Chapter 3

MISMANAGED, RIGGED, AND DISGRACED

Some sports fails are made on such a large scale that they impact the course of the entire game. Cheating scandals, while shameful, end up making the game safer and fairer. Some mistakes are the first step in a long line of decisions that lead to another team's fortune. And yet others feature a lapse in judgment that has a long-lasting effect.

Babe Ruth starred as a pitcher for the Boston Red Sox.

The Curse of the Bambino

Harry Frazee bought the champion Boston Red Sox in 1916 and saw them through a few tough years. Under financial stress in 1919, he chose to sell up-and-coming star Babe Ruth to the New York Yankees for $100,000.

On his new team, Ruth switched from pitcher to

outfielder and became one of the game's greatest hitters. After trading Ruth, the Red Sox didn't win a World Series title for eighty-six years. Fans called it the Curse of the Bambino (Ruth's nickname). In that time, Frazee traded away even more of his players, while the Yankees became the winningest team in baseball with twenty-six championships.

After the Red Sox sold Ruth to the New York Yankees, he became one of the greatest hitters in baseball history.

The Chicago Black Sox

Perhaps the most famous instance of large-scale cheating in sports came at the same time that Harry Frazee was trading Babe Ruth. In Chicago, a group of eight White Sox players decided that they would lose the 1919 World Series on purpose. Professional gamblers bet on the games and paid the players for losing.

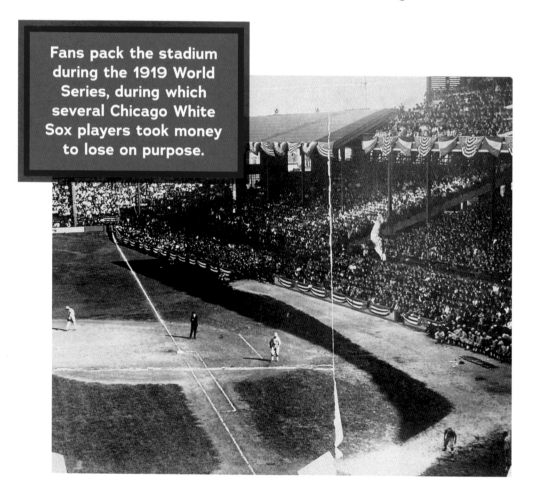

Fans pack the stadium during the 1919 World Series, during which several Chicago White Sox players took money to lose on purpose.

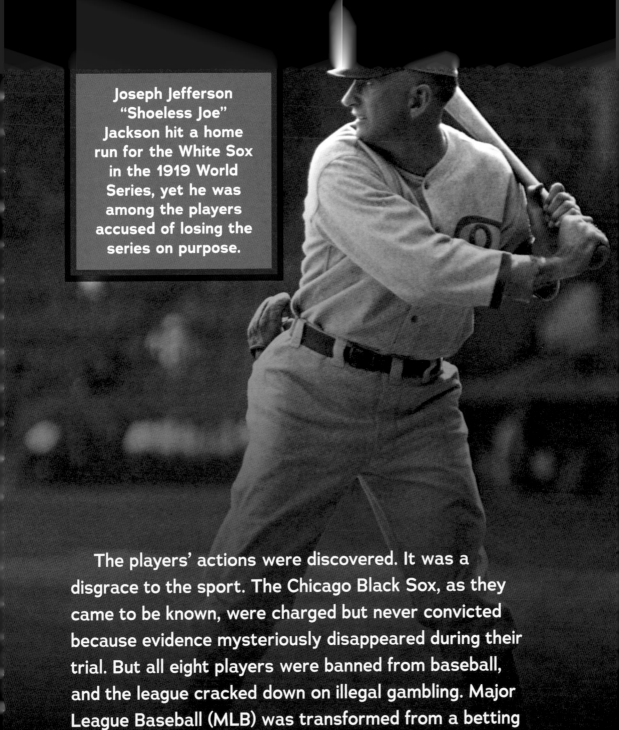

Joseph Jefferson "Shoeless Joe" Jackson hit a home run for the White Sox in the 1919 World Series, yet he was among the players accused of losing the series on purpose.

The players' actions were discovered. It was a disgrace to the sport. The Chicago Black Sox, as they came to be known, were charged but never convicted because evidence mysteriously disappeared during their trial. But all eight players were banned from baseball, and the league cracked down on illegal gambling. Major League Baseball (MLB) was transformed from a betting

The Disgrace of Gijón

It was the final game of the group stage at the 1982 World Cup in Gijon, Spain. West Germany was playing Austria. Based on their standings in the group, and complex tie-breaker rules, a close game could allow both teams to move into the knockout stage at the expense of underdog Algeria.

A German defender stops an Austrian attack early in their 1982 World Cup match. Once Germany took a 1-0 lead, both teams appeared to stop trying to score.

Fans jeer German forward Karl-Heinz Rummenigge as he walks off the field.

West Germany scored within the first ten minutes, and then both teams stopped playing competitively for the remaining eighty. Boos filled the stadium as fans figured out what the teams were doing. They had clearly agreed to fix the score, but FIFA found no clear evidence that the game was rigged. They did, however, change the rules of the World Cup so that the last two games of the group stage were played at the same time, so no team could base their game play on another's results.

Chapter 4

THE TWELFTH MAN

In sports with eleven players on the field (such as football and soccer), the Twelfth Man is the name for the fans, recognizing the role they play in the success of teams. That means they can be equally responsible for a team's failure. Whether they interfere with play, run through the field, or otherwise disturb players and coaches, fans are no strangers to sports fails.

Seattle Seahawks fans at Super Bowl XLVIII hold up a banner standing for the Twelfth Man.

Fans Foul It Up

No fan is better known for spoiling a game than Steve Bartman. The die-hard Cubs fan was in the stands for game 6 of the 2003 National League Championship Series. The Cubs were ahead 3–0 in the eighth inning, just a few outs away from making it to the World Series.

Chicago Cubs fan Steve Bartman reaches out in an attempt to catch a foul ball. His interference prevents outfielder Moises Alou from catching the ball.

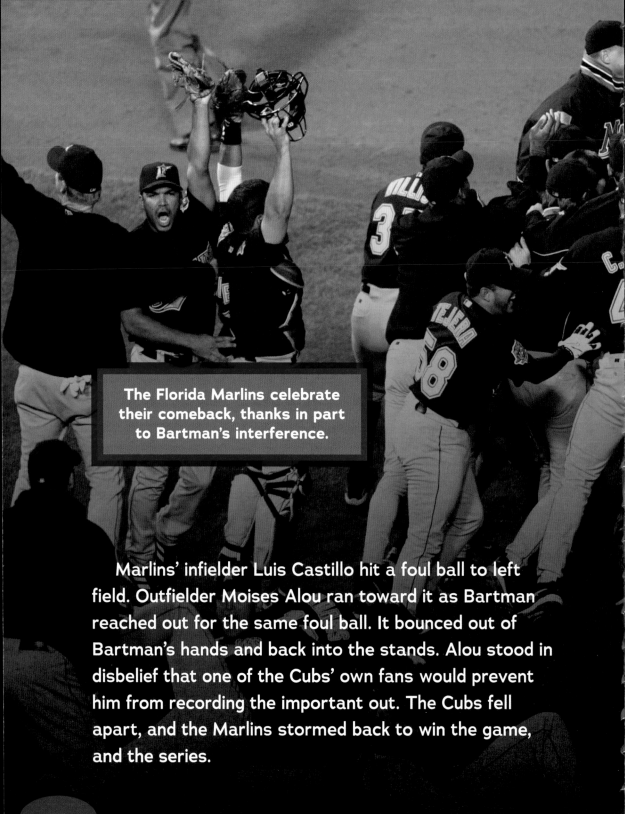

The Florida Marlins celebrate their comeback, thanks in part to Bartman's interference.

Marlins' infielder Luis Castillo hit a foul ball to left field. Outfielder Moises Alou ran toward it as Bartman reached out for the same foul ball. It bounced out of Bartman's hands and back into the stands. Alou stood in disbelief that one of the Cubs' own fans would prevent him from recording the important out. The Cubs fell apart, and the Marlins stormed back to win the game, and the series.

The Cubs celebrate their success at the 2016 World Series championship ring ceremony.

For a long time, fans and players blamed Bartman for the loss. It got so bad that Bartman went into hiding. Most fans eventually forgave him. The Cubs even presented him with his own World Series ring when the team finally won in 2016.

The Horns Heard round the World

The 2010 World Cup was hosted by South Africa, in the capital city of Johannesburg. It introduced the world to their fans' favorite cheering tool: the vuvuzela. The loud horn found its way into soccer stadiums, and the hearts of South African fans.

Fans blow into cheap, plastic vuvuzelas at the 2010 World Cup in South Africa.

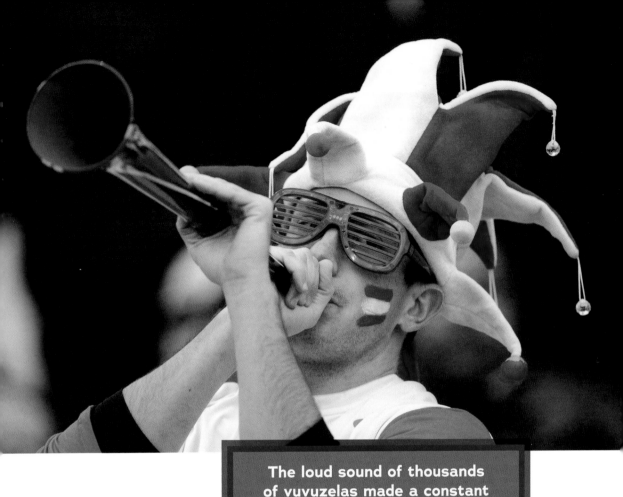

The loud sound of thousands of vuvuzelas made a constant buzzing at the 2010 World Cup. FIFA later banned the instruments.

During play, South African arenas were drowned out by the wailing of cheap, plastic vuvuzelas. Their constant droning was criticized by fans, viewers, players, and commentators alike. For the 2014 World Cup, FIFA made sure to include vuvuzelas on their list of banned items, to the relief of many.

Failure Isn't the End

When it comes to failing at sports, everyone does it at one point or another, even world champions and Olympic medalists. But most are able to shake it off and return to their peak performance. For them, failure is a way to learn and improve their games.

The Stanford band streams onto the field in 1982. They were celebrating what they believed to be a Stanford victory over Cal. Moments later, Cal scored the game-winning touchdown.

Failing Upward

In 1982, Stanford and the University of California, Berkeley (Cal), faced off in the "Big Game." Stanford was up 20–19 with four seconds left to play. Victory was within reach. On the final play, the Stanford band began filing onto the field to help celebrate the big win. But Cal managed to pull off a miracle kick return, weaving through the stunned band members on the way to score the game-winning touchdown. This messy, improbable, and totally absurd play is one of the most memorable moments in college sports history.

Cal players celebrate their amazing comeback victory over Stanford in 1982.

Glossary

criticize: to find and point out faults or problems

drop: the placing of a golf ball onto a designated area after it has been lost to a water hazard

interception: the act of a defensive player catching a forward pass

method grab: in board sports, grabbing the heel of the board while in air, twisting, and then landing facing forward

rigged: prearranged so that the winner is decided before the competition

scapegoat: a person who is blamed for the wrongdoings, mistakes, or faults of others

synonymous: closely associated with or suggestive of something

underdog: the person or team that is not favored to win

Learn More about Sports Fails

Books

Doeden, Matt. *Coming Up Clutch: The Greatest Upsets, Comebacks, Finishes in Sports History.* Minneapolis: Millbrook Press, 2019. Learn more about the teams and players who made (or missed) important plays in sports' biggest games.

Sports Illustrated Kids editors. *Big Book of Who: All-Stars.* New York: Time Home Entertainment, 2014. Get the scoop on all your favorite players, teams, and all-around champions.

Zuckerman, Gregory, Elijah Zuckerman, and Gabriel Zuckerman. *Rising Above: How 11 Athletes Overcame Challenges in Their Youth to Become Stars.* New York: Philomel Books, 2016 Take a deeper look at what it takes to train and become a professional athlete.

Websites

Dogo News
https://www.dogonews.com/category/sports
Stay in tune with all the latest sports news, plus view profiles on important players throughout history.

100 Biggest Blunders in Sports History
https://bleacherreport.com/articles/598620-100-biggest-blunders-in-sports-history#slide0
Read even more about all the ways that players, managers, coaches, and fans have messed up over the years.

Sports Illustrated Kids
https://www.sikids.com/
Stay up-to-date on all your favorite players, sports, and big games, and read articles written by and about other kids.

...and

...ck Sox, 18–19

...razee, Harry, 17–18

Houston Oilers, 4–6

Jacobellis, Lindsey, 15

New York Yankees, 17

Olympics, 15

Ruth, Babe, 16–18

Stanford, 28–29

University of California, Berkeley, 28–29

Van de Velde, Jean, 12–14

vuvuzela, 26–27

Wilson, Mookie, 9

World Cup, 20–21, 26–27

World Series, 8–9, 17–19, 23, 25

Photo Acknowledgments

Image credits: AP Photo/Al Messerschmidt, p. 4; AP Photo/Bill Sikes, p. 5; AP Photo/Chuck Solomon, p. 6; Bob Martin/Getty Images, p. 7; AP Photo/G. Paul Burnett, p. 8; Focus on Sport/Getty Images, p. 9; Boston Globe/Getty Images, p. 10; AP Photo/Rusty Kennedy, p. 11; Andrew Redington /Getty Images, p. 12; Phil Sheldon/Popperfoto/Getty Images, pp. 13, 14; Joe Rimkus Jr./Miami Herald/MCT/Getty Images, p. 15; Library of Congress, p. 16; Mark Rucker/Transcendental Graphics/Getty Images, p. 17; APA/Getty Images, p. 18; Corbis/Getty Images, p. 19; picture alliance/Getty Images, p. 20; Mönckebild/picture alliance/Getty Images, p. 21; Christian Petersen /Getty Images, p. 22; AP Photo/Morry Gash, p. 23; Elsa/Getty Images, p. 24; AP Photo/Matt Marton, p. 25; Clive Rose/Getty Images, p. 26; John MacDougall/AFP/Getty Images, p. 27; AP Photo/Carl Viti, pp. 28, 29.

Cover: Tetra Images/Getty Images.